Contents

Fast 4

Slow 6

Fast and slow 8

Boats and ships 10

Motorbikes and bicycles 12

Cheetahs and tortoises 14

Horses 16

Running and walking 18

Racing at the beach 20

Fast or slow? 22

Index 24

Notes for adults 24

Fast

This is a racing car.

It is very *fast*.

Slow

This is a steamroller.
It is **slow**.

Fast and slow

This is a rocket blasting into space.

Is it fast or slow?

This is a tractor on a farm.

Is it fast
or slow?

Boats and ships

This is a speedboat on a lake.

This is a big ship on the sea.

The speedboat is **faster** than the ship.

Motorbikes and bicycles

This motorbike has a big engine.

This bicycle has no engine at all.

Which is *faster*, the motorbike or the bicycle?

Cheetahs and tortoises

This is a cheetah.
It is running very *fast*.

This is a tortoise.

It is walking very **slowly**.

Horses

This horse is running. Is it moving **fast** or **slowly**?

This horse is walking. Is it moving
fast or **slowly?**

Running and walking

These women are running very *fast*.

This woman is running the *fastest*.

These people are walking **slowly**.

This girl is walking the **slowest**.

Racing at the beach

These children are racing each other at the beach.

Who is moving the *fastest*?

Who is moving the **slowest**?

Fast or slow?

Can you remember what was *fast* and what was **slow**?

23

Index

beach 20

bicycle 12

cheetah. 14

horse 16, 17

motorbike 12

people. 18, 19

racing car 4

rocket 8

ship 11

speedboat 10, 11

steamroller 6

tortoise 15

tractor 9

Notes for adults

The *How Do Things Move?* series provides young children with a first opportunity to learn about motion. Each book encourages children to notice and ask questions about the types of movement they see around them. The following Early Learning Goals are relevant to the series:

Knowledge and understanding of the world
• Find out about and identify some features of living things and objects
• Ask questions about why things happen and how things work
• Show an interest in the world in which they live
• Encourage use of evaluative and comparative language

These books will also help children extend their vocabulary, as they will hear some new words. Since words are used in context in the book this should enable young children to gradually incorporate them into their own vocabulary.

Follow-up activities
• Help your child improve his or her numerical ability by asking them to think of ten things that are fast and ten things that are slow.
• Develop your child's comparative skills by choosing three things from the book and then asking them to list them in order of speed.